Original title:
Letters Unsent

Copyright © 2024 Swan Charm
All rights reserved.

Author: Olivia Oja
ISBN HARDBACK: 978-9916-79-261-2
ISBN PAPERBACK: 978-9916-79-262-9
ISBN EBOOK: 978-9916-79-263-6

Sacred Refuge of Unwritten Words

In shadows deep where whispers lie,
The heart seeks solace, soft and nigh.
An altar built of hopes and dreams,
Each silent prayer, a flowing stream.

Beneath the stars, in night's embrace,
We find a truth, a holy space.
Words left unspoken, yet they soar,
In sacred refuge, we explore.

With every breath, the spirit cries,
For light and love beyond the skies.
In silence, we shall find our grace,
In unwritten words, a warm embrace.

The echoes linger, soft and clear,
A gentle touch, a cosmic sphere.
Together bound by unseen threads,
In unity, where divinity spreads.

Each moment cherished, pure and bright,
In sacred realms, we unite.
The unwritten paths, our hearts now tread,
In love's embrace, our spirits spread.

The Divine Silence Between Us

In quietude where angels tread,
A space divine, where hopes are fed.
The whispers of the soul's own song,
In stillness found, where we belong.

Between the lines of every prayer,
A tender pause, a love laid bare.
In silence deep, we hear the call,
The gentle sigh of grace for all.

The heartbeat of the night unfolds,
In sacred trust, our spirits hold.
The love that lives in what's not said,
In silence bound, we're gently led.

With eyes that meet, yet words undone,
In tender warmth, two hearts are one.
The sacred space, a bridge we cross,
In every silence, gain through loss.

The light that glows within the void,
In every pause, our faith deployed.
Together we shall navigate,
The divine silence, our true state.

Reflections in the Mirror of Faith

In stillness, I gaze upon my soul,
Seeking the light that makes me whole.
Each whisper of doubt, a shadow cast,
Yet in grace, I find peace at last.

Truth lingers softly in sacred air,
Guiding my heart with gentle care.
In trials faced, I see Him near,
A presence that calms all deeply held fear.

The mirror reflects my earnest plea,
To walk in light, to truly see.
With each prayer, my spirit lifts,
In faith, I find my greatest gifts.

Here in silence, wisdom unfolds,
Stories of love through ages told.
A tapestry woven with threads of grace,
In every trial, I see His face.

In every moment, faith holds fast,
A foundation that will forever last.
Through valleys deep and mountains high,
My spirit soars, my heart will fly.

Non-Verbal Testaments of Love

In actions quiet, a love declared,
In gestures simple, hearts unpaired.
A smile exchanged, a knowing glance,
In silent grace, we share our dance.

Hands reaching out, no words required,
In warmth and touch, our souls conspired.
Every kindness, a testament true,
A bond unbroken, me and you.

Through trials faced, we stand as one,
In patient strength, our battles won.
Though words may falter, hearts will speak,
In moments shared, we find the peak.

A laughter shared under the stars,
In unison, we heal our scars.
With every heartbeat, love does grow,
In the quiet places, peace we sow.

In our eyes, a story told,
Of love enduring, brave and bold.
Silent vows that time can't sever,
In this testament, we live forever.

The Altar of Unsent Conversations

Upon this altar, thoughts reside,
Words unspoken, feelings hide.
In whispers caught, a longing sigh,
Every silence, a heartfelt cry.

Memories linger in the air,
Of things we meant, our hopes laid bare.
Each thought a prayer, a dream delayed,
In this haven, our love portrayed.

In echoes deep, our voices blend,
Conversations held, yet never penned.
A tapestry of what could be,
In every pause, your soul speaks to me.

The beauty found in what's unsaid,
In quiet moments, we are led.
Beyond the noise, our spirits meet,
In sacred silence, love is sweet.

With every breath, we honor the space,
Where unsent words embrace our grace.
An altar built on trust and care,
In love's embrace, we find our prayer.

Hushed Annunciations of the Soul

In hushed tones, the spirit stirs,
Whispers carried on gentle purrs.
Each breath a note, a sacred hymn,
In stillness, our faith begins to swim.

At dawn's light, the world awakes,
With quiet joy, my heart partakes.
In the soft glow, I find my voice,
In every silence, the soul's choice.

Through shadows cast by doubt and fear,
A whispered calling, ever near.
Each heartbeat echoes love untold,
A divine promise, bright and bold.

In fervent prayers, the soul ascends,
With every sigh, the spirit mends.
Anointing grace in daily roles,
Hushed annunciations of our souls.

In twilight's peace, reflections gleam,
In whispered love, we find our dream.
Through silent night, our hearts will soar,
In quiet faith, forevermore.

Words to the Uncreated

In silence deep, the spirit calls,
To realms beyond where no time falls.
The whisper of love, eternally free,
Awakens the heart, brings forth the plea.

Light pierces night, the darkness frayed,
In sacred space where fears are laid.
Words of the ancients, forever pure,
Guide us to love, the only cure.

From voids unknown, creation speaks,
A symphony rare, where glory peaks.
In every breath, a promise shines,
In heart's embrace, the divine aligns.

With hands uplifted, we seek the grace,
Of truth bestowed in our humble place.
To the Uncreated, we bow and sing,
As echoes of hope in our souls take wing.

Eulogy for the Unsent

In twilight's hush, we gather here,
For words unspoken, yet held dear.
The unsent dreams that never took flight,
In hearts they linger, a quiet light.

A letter penned in the depths of night,
Whispers of love, a soul's delight.
Yet tucked away, without a chance,
We mourn the loss of a sweet romance.

Unwritten vows upon the page,
Now echo softly, void of age.
In silent sorrow, we stand as one,
For hopes that flickered but never shone.

Yet in the absence, we find a grace,
In each heartbeat, a tender trace.
The unsent words, now freed from bind,
Eternal whispers, forever entwined.

The Diary of Inexpressible Love

In pages worn, with ink of dreams,
The heart confides, or so it seems.
This diary holds the joys and woes,
Of love profound that ever flows.

With each soft stroke, the essence spills,
Of moments shared, of heart's true thrills.
In laughter's bloom and tearful sighs,
A tapestry weaves 'neath wide-open skies.

Yet words fall short of the depth we know,
For love transcends all earthly flow.
In glances brief and tender touch,
We find the essence; we've said so much.

Dear diary, keeper of secrets vast,
In your embrace, our shadows cast.
For inexpressible love finds a way,
To linger still, come what may.

Enlightened Thoughts Never Spoken

In quietude, the mind does roam,
Seeking truths that feel like home.
Thoughts of light, in shadows cast,
Whisper wisdom: hold steadfast.

What's left unvoiced, yet deeply felt,
In sacred silence, love is dealt.
A universe vast, inside we find,
Enlightened whispers, hearts aligned.

Each gentle breath, a chance to see,
The beauty of what's yet to be.
In the stillness, answers lie,
Awaiting those with open sky.

Though words may falter, hearts will speak,
In the light we seek, it's truth we seek.
In thoughts unshared, we find our grace,
Enlightened paths, a shared embrace.

Odes to the Silent

In quietude, the spirit finds peace,
Whispers of grace in the gentle breeze.
Angels listen with hearts made of light,
Each hushed prayer takes sacred flight.

The stillness speaks of the love divine,
In moments of silence, our souls entwine.
Echoes of faith in the night unfold,
Stories of mercy, eternally told.

Through shadows, the light begins to gleam,
In the absence of noise, we dare to dream.
A chorus of hearts, a symphony bright,
In honor of silence, we take to flight.

Reverent Longing in the Void

In the depths of absence, longing blooms,
A sacred ache in the quiet rooms.
Stars whisper secrets to the dark air,
In every heartbeat, a silent prayer.

The cosmos sighs with each fleeting breath,
Life dances softly upon the path of death.
In shadows, we find what words can't convey,
A reverent longing that won't fade away.

Emptiness cradles the dreams we've spun,
In the vastness, we find we're never done.
Graceful echoes fill the void of regret,
In faith, we rise, our souls firmly met.

Chronology of Unsaid Goodbyes

Time drips slowly, a painful refrain,
Each unsaid word a lingering chain.
Moments pass by with heavy sighs,
Echoes of love in unsaid goodbyes.

Seasons change but the heart stays true,
Memories linger of all that we knew.
What we hold close in heart's quiet bays,
Speak volumes in silence, through twilight haze.

A timeline woven of laughter and tears,
Words left unspoken, harbored fears.
Yet still, we cherish the bonds that ignite,
In the depth of silence, we find the light.

Rites of the Unexpressed

Beneath the surface, emotions reside,
In the spaces where our hopes abide.
Rituals whispered in the softest tones,
Embracing the heart, the soul's hidden zones.

With each heartbeat, a story unfolds,
Silent confessions in the tales we hold.
In the quiet embrace of the unseen,
Lies the truth of what may have been.

Gathering shadows, we raise our vow,
For every sorrow, we honor the now.
In rites of the unexpressed, we find grace,
A sanctuary carved from the silent space.

Messages of the Soul in Limbo

In shadows soft, the whispers call,
A journey sought beyond the wall.
Echoes brush against the night,
Souls linger still, caught in the light.

The gates of dawn, a fleeting dream,
A hope that flows like a silver stream.
Hear the songs of those who wait,
In silent prayer, they contemplate.

A tapestry of lives once lived,
In love and loss, the heart forgives.
Each thread a tale, a sacred part,
In limbo's grace, they share their heart.

With every breath, the spirit sighs,
A soft lament beneath the skies.
Finding peace in the still unknown,
For every soul, a place called home.

The Unwritten Gospels

In every heart, a truth concealed,
A sacred text that time has sealed.
Words unspoken, lives unsung,
The gospels wait, forever young.

Each moment speaks of love and pain,
In silent prayers, the lost remain.
From dust to dust, the faith holds fast,
In shadows cast, the die is cast.

Through trials faced and battles fought,
The lessons learned, through pain are taught.
A beacon shines within the dark,
In every life, a holy spark.

The pages turn, but we must write,
Our stories etched in the endless night.
These unwritten gospels find their voice,
In every heart, we make the choice.

Testaments Lost in the Ether

In whispers soft, the echoes cry,
Testaments drift where shadows lie.
A breeze of faith, a sigh of grace,
Lost in the ether, we seek our place.

Beyond the veil, the truths await,
In timeless realms, we navigate.
Stories woven in the stars,
Mirrored in the moonlight's scars.

When silence speaks, our spirits yearn,
A quest for love, we seek and learn.
Each testament, a spark divine,
In fractured light, our souls align.

From ashes rise the tales we tell,
In every wound, a sacred shell.
To walk the path of those before,
In lost testaments, we explore.

Ghosts of the Untold

In shadowed halls, where echoes wane,
Ghosts of the untold haunt the lane.
With every step, we feel their weight,
In sighs of time, they resonate.

Stories cloaked in mist and fear,
Unraveled threads that draw us near.
Each ghost a witness, standing tall,
To every rise, and every fall.

Their voices linger, soft and low,
Tales of love and seeds we sow.
In every heart, a specter dwells,
With breath immortal, they weave their spells.

From shadow's grasp, their light will shine,
In untold paths, the souls align.
Guiding us through the vale of night,
Ghosts of the untold, eternal light.

The Quietude of Longing Hearts

In the stillness, whispers sigh,
Hearts beat softly, prayers rise high.
In shadows cast by faith's embrace,
Yearning souls find their own space.

Beneath the stars, a silence deep,
In every longing, faith does seep.
The quietude, a gentle guide,
In hope's embrace, we will abide.

Oh, sacred calm in night's expanse,
Each heartbeat sings a fervent dance.
In seeking grace, our spirits soar,
For in the stillness, we explore.

A longing bridge to what's divine,
Hearts entwined in love's design.
Each breath a vow to seek the light,
In quietude, we share our plight.

Thus we unite in fervent dreams,
Where faith flows forth in gentle streams.
Hearts that ache and souls that yearn,
In silent worship, we discern.

The Celestial Query Unanswered

Upon the heavens, questions rise,
The echoes float through endless skies.
In starry realms, we seek a sign,
Yet wisdom dances, sly and fine.

The moon conceals a secret glow,
In night's embrace, our longings flow.
What lies beyond our fleeting sight?
In silent query, we chase light.

Each heart a vessel, longing deep,
Guarding truths that we must keep.
Celestial whispers, soft and clear,
Yet answers fade, as dreams appear.

In sacred stillness, shadows blend,
Searching for where the journey ends.
Who holds the key to our desire?
In questions deep, our thoughts conspire.

Thus we ponder, souls in flight,
Ciphers lost within the night.
With every breath, our spirits yearn,
In an unanswered prayer, we learn.

Emissaries of the Unstated Desires

We walk the paths of unspoken need,
Beneath each star, our souls proceed.
With every glance, a story spins,
In quiet realms, where love begins.

Emissaries of hearts so brave,
In whispered hopes, the light we crave.
Each unvoiced wish, a prayer set free,
In silent bonds, our spirits see.

The seasons turn, yet still we seek,
Voices soft, the soul's mystique.
Through every trial, we refine,
The essence sacred, pure, divine.

In gardens bright, our longings grow,
The winds of change, they come and go.
With gentle grace, we pave the way,
For unconfessed dreams that softly sway.

Embracing truths in tender light,
We share our journeys, day and night.
As emissaries of the heart,
Together we shall never part.

Celestial Ciphers of the Heart

In the tapestry of twilight's glow,
Celestial ciphers gently flow.
Each heartbeat holds a secret score,
In tender rhythms, we explore.

Stars above in silent flight,
Illuminate the paths of light.
In whispered prayers, our souls connect,
Where love and longing gently intersect.

Every sigh a coded plea,
In sacred echoes, hearts run free.
Through veils of night, we seek the key,
To unlock the depths, our spirits flee.

The cosmos speaks in sacred signs,
In every glance, divinity twines.
As whispers weave through endless space,
In ciphers soft, we find our grace.

In quietude, our spirits learn,
Through every twist, the stars we yearn.
Celestial hearts in cadence beat,
In love's language, we are complete.

Prayers Not Said

In silence, hearts do call,
Yearning for the light,
Echoes of whispers small,
Lost within the night.

Hands clasped in tender grace,
Hope's shadowed embrace,
Seeking a divine face,
In this sacred space.

Stars witness our fear,
Like lanterns in the gloom,
Each unspoken tear,
Nurtures faith to bloom.

In the stillness we find,
The strength to hold on tight,
Binding heart and mind,
In the eternal fight.

Though the words may fail,
The spirit shall prevail,
Leaving a holy trail,
Where love will not curtail.

Whispers of Faith Uncarved

Beyond the stone and clay,
Lives a voice so pure,
In the dawn's warm ray,
Faith, forever sure.

Unseen, yet so alive,
In the breeze, it flows,
A gentle nudge to strive,
In the heart, it grows.

Mountains bow in grace,
To the whispering sound,
Of a wise embrace,
Where love is unbound.

Through trials and despair,
Hope's light breaks through,
In the quiet air,
Faith whispers anew.

To the weary soul,
It offers a spark,
A promise made whole,
In the endless dark.

Scripts of Celestial Longing

On parchment of the skies,
Written dreams take flight,
Where the spirit lies,
Chasing realms of light.

In cosmic ink and fire,
Each wish finds its way,
Scribing deep desire,
In the dance of day.

The heavens breathe a song,
For those who seek the truth,
In this world so strong,
We find our shared youth.

Words penned with the stars,
Guide us through the night,
Healing all our scars,
With each beam of light.

Life whispers in time,
From the heavens above,
In rhythm and rhyme,
Tales of endless love.

Memories in the Ether

In the quietia of still,
Echoes softly dwell,
Where time bends its will,
And all stories tell.

Fragments of lost days,
Carried on the breeze,
Like sweet summer's rays,
Bring the soul to ease.

Threads that weave our fate,
Bind heart to the past,
In the hands of fate,
Our shadows are cast.

Gathered in the light,
Are places we have known,
In the still of night,
We search for our own.

Every whisper holds grace,
In the ether's warm glow,
In time's soft embrace,
Love will always flow.

Prayers on the Wind

In the hush of dawn's embrace,
Soft whispers reach the skies,
Hearts uplifted, seeking grace,
As the morning light does rise.

Gentle breezes carry hope,
Each prayer a floating song,
Through the valleys, wide they scope,
To know where we belong.

Leaves rustle in sacred dance,
Nature's hymn, a soul's delight,
In a moment's fleeting chance,
We find love and pure insight.

Carry forth our humble dreams,
Like petals cast on streams of thought,
In silence, hear the sacred themes,
In each breath, our wishes caught.

Let us gather in this space,
Where our souls in whispers blend,
With the world, we find our place,
In the prayers that never end.

Unspoken Blessings

In quiet moments, blessings flow,
Words unuttered, deeply felt,
Through the heart, where kindness grows,
Each gesture, a love that's knelt.

Silent rivers, wisdom's grace,
Unseen hands that guide our way,
With each heartbeat, we embrace,
Solar light to lead the day.

Softened glances, gentle smiles,
Embrace the world in care,
Through the trials, through the miles,
Faith unfolds, forever rare.

In the space 'twixt breath and sigh,
Every heartbeat tells a tale,
Invisible threads that tie,
In unity, we shall prevail.

Let us weave a tapestry,
Of hopes stitched deep in silence,
In unspoken ecstasy,
Where we find our true alliance.

The Altar of Words

Upon the altar, truths reside,
With every phrase, a sacred spark,
In voice and silence, we abide,
Illuminating the deep dark.

Words like candles, softly glow,
Guiding souls through night's embrace,
Each syllable, a lover's flow,
In this space, we find our grace.

Pages turn in whispered prayer,
Lessons learned through trials faced,
Ink flows freely, as we share,
In the stories, wisdom laced.

Lifted high, our hopes unite,
In verses crafted with intent,
With every rise, we take to flight,
Our hearts in harmony, content.

Beneath this arch of light divine,
We gather all our human plight,
In the sacred space we find,
The power of our shared insight.

Communion of Unwritten Sentiments

In the quiet, hearts connect,
Feelings shared without a sound,
In the depths, our souls reflect,
Where true warmth and peace abound.

Whispers linger in the air,
Unsung hymns of love and care,
From the light, a heartfelt prayer,
Binding us with every share.

In the pauses, meaning grows,
Every glance, a sacred rite,
In the depths of silence flows,
A gentle touch, a guiding light.

With the breath of every thought,
We weave a bond of hope and trust,
In this sacred place we've sought,
Unwritten blessings, pure and just.

Together we will move as one,
In harmony, our spirits soar,
With unspoken words, we run,
To the open, loving shore.

Reflections of the Heart Untold

In shadows deep, where whispers dwell,
The heart confides its secret swell.
Each thought a prayer, each sigh a grace,
In silence held, we find our place.

With every tear, a lesson learned,
In trials faced, the spirit burned.
Through faith we walk, though paths be steep,
In sacred trust, the soul will reap.

The light that flickers, dim yet bright,
Guides the way through darkest night.
Each ember glows with love's embrace,
In every heartbeat, seek His face.

The echoes fade, yet still they ring,
A melody of hope, we sing.
In every doubt, let courage rise,
For in the heart, the truth belies.

Untold the stories we must weave,
In silent prayers, our hearts believe.
With every step on this unknown road,
We find the strength in love bestowed.

The Quiet Testament of the Heart

In the stillness where spirits meet,
Whispers linger, soft and sweet.
The heart's testament gently glows,
In every pulse, His presence shows.

Amidst the chaos, peace abides,
In faith's embrace, the heart confides.
Each longing sigh, a sacred song,
In softest tones, we find where we belong.

Through storms of life, we stand our ground,
In every loss, the grace is found.
With open hearts, we seek the light,
In the quiet, love ignites.

In each reflection, wisdom grows,
A tapestry of joy and woes.
In cadence soft, our spirits soar,
To the rhythm of the love we bore.

Trust in the journey, unfulfilled,
In every moment, hope is stilled.
With steadfast hearts, we journey on,
The quiet testament, our hearts' song.

Unsealed Confessions to the Divine

In whispered tones, we raise our plea,
In humble hearts, we long to see.
Each confession, a secret shared,
In open arms, the soul is bared.

The burdens we carry, laid to rest,
In sacred space, we find our quest.
Through shadows cast, the light will break,
In tender grace, our spirits wake.

With every question, answers bloom,
In struggles faced, dispelling gloom.
The heart unsealed, a radiant glow,
In love's embrace, we truly grow.

Each joy we seek, a call divine,
In gratitude, our hearts align.
Through every trial that makes us whole,
We find the thread that binds the soul.

So let us speak in truth and grace,
To the Divine, we find our place.
In unsealed confessions, hope is cast,
In love's embrace, we'll ever last.

Pilgrimage of Untold Words

With every step upon this path,
We tread in faith, and silence hath.
A pilgrimage of soul's intent,
In every heartbeat, love is sent.

The road is long, yet hearts are bold,
In stories whispered, truth unfolds.
Each untold word, a beacon bright,
In darkest hours, they bring the light.

Through valleys low and mountains high,
In silent prayers, our spirits fly.
With open hands, we walk in grace,
In unity, we seek His face.

The journey's song, both sweet and clear,
With every note, we draw Him near.
In hopes unspoken, dreams collide,
In pilgrimage, our hearts abide.

So let us wander, let us roam,
In every heart, we find our home.
Through untold words, the truth will sound,
In love's embrace, our souls are found.

Scripts of the Unwritten

In silent echoes, words await,
Beneath the stars, we contemplate.
In humble hearts, they long to rise,
Unfolding truths beneath the skies.

Each breath a note in heaven's choir,
A whispered prayer, a burning fire.
In shadows deep, the spirit speaks,
Guiding us through all that peaks.

The pages blank, yet filled with grace,
For in our souls, the dreams we trace.
In stillness found, divinity flows,
From quiet seeds, the virtue grows.

The ink of fate, forever runs,
We pen the light of distant suns.
With faith as ink, our stories start,
Awakening love within the heart.

The Divine Drafts

From heights above, a vision clear,
The drafts descend, we hold them dear.
In every line, a promise made,
In sacred light, our path is laid.

Eternal whispers guide our hands,
As we weave hope through ancient strands.
With every stroke, a tale unfolds,
Revealing mysteries of old.

The parchment trembles with the lore,
Of countries lost, and ancient war.
In harmony, the voices blend,
A testament that time won't end.

As drafts drift softly through the night,
Their gentle glow, a soul's delight.
With love embedded in the text,
We find the truths we never vexed.

Edicts Lost in Time

In crumbling scrolls, the edicts lie,
With wisdom deep, they reach the sky.
A sacred mandate, etched with care,
For those who seek, the truth laid bare.

Among the ruins, voices call,
A distant echo, a ancient thrall.
Each binding word, a call to lean,
On faith as strong as walls unseen.

Through centuries, the shadows weave,
In quiet prayer, we learn to believe.
The lost commands, we now retrieve,
In every heart, new worlds conceive.

With every breath, the past is clear,
The echoes drum, they draw us near.
In the silence, wisdom chimes,
To guide our steps through lost eras' rhymes.

Murmurs of Sacred Hope

In whispered tones, the night reveals,
The sacred hope that softly heals.
Among the stars, our dreams take flight,
In unity, we seek the light.

The fragile thread that time can weave,
Connects all hearts who dare believe.
From depths of night, a dawn will rise,
With love and faith as our allies.

In every breath, a story spun,
Of faith undying, and battles won.
The murmurs flow like gentle streams,
Quenching the thirst of shattered dreams.

Through trials fierce, we stand as one,
In sacred hope, our battle's won.
With every pulse, the promise glows,
In harmony, the spirit grows.

Missives from the Ether

In the silence of the night,
Whispers dance like gentle light.
From above, a call we hear,
Messages sent, crystal clear.

Angels weave their secret thread,
In the void where dreams are fed.
Voices rise as shadows fall,
In sacred echoes, we stand small.

The stars, they twinkle with grace,
Guiding us through time and space.
Each pulse a note, divine and sweet,
Drawing us to the holy beat.

Listen closely, hearts awake,
In every breath, a vow we make.
The ether sings, a tranquil song,
Inviting souls to join along.

A tapestry of love and light,
Unfolds before our seeking sight.
In the stillness, faith ignites,
Leading us through endless nights.

The Eternal Echo of Words

Words once spoken, never fade,
In the hearts where love is laid.
Across the ages, truth resounds,
In every soul, the spirit found.

From prophets' lips, a fire burns,
A sacred message, the heart yearns.
Each verse a thread in time's great loom,
Weaving light to scatter gloom.

In quiet places, truth will rise,
Reflecting dreams in open skies.
An echo of the sacred past,
In whispered prayers, our faith holds fast.

The tongue of angels softly speaks,
Illuminating paths, though bleak.
Through trials fierce, our voices blend,
A harmony that will not end.

Through holy whispers, wisdom flows,
In every rapture, love still grows.
These words, a bridge to realms unseen,
Connecting all that might have been.

Sermons in Empty Spaces

In barren fields, the spirit stirs,
Where silence reigns, the heart concurs.
In empty rooms, we find our prayer,
A sacred bond, a love to share.

Echoes linger, soft and true,
In solitude, we find the hue.
The light shines bright in darkest night,
Guided by faith, we take our flight.

A whisper speaks to those who stray,
Calling back to the righteous way.
In gentle tones, the truth unfolds,
A sermon of love that never folds.

In the quiet, we seek the sound,
Where creation's voice can be found.
Each moment of stillness, divine,
A chance to glimpse the great design.

With open hearts, we learn to see,
The beauty in our sacred plea.
In every void, a love embraced,
In empty spaces, grace is traced.

Messages on the Wings of Time

Time, a river, swift and wide,
Carries messages on its tide.
Each moment, a bird takes flight,
Soaring forth into the night.

Like doves, they bear our hopes and dreams,
In gentle streams with sacred themes.
Through ages past, their whispers weave,
An invitation to believe.

On every breeze, a story tells,
Of truths that time softly impels.
In shadows cast and glimmers bright,
Love remains, our guiding light.

In every tear, a lesson learned,
In every joy, the heart has yearned.
Through years that fade, faith holds its place,
In timeless love's warm embrace.

As seasons change, and years go by,
Messages lift us, let us fly.
With open hearts, we rise and climb,
Embraced by grace on wings of time.

Gospels Left in the Abyss

In shadows deep, where whispers fade,
The gospels lost, in silence laid.
Beneath the weight of time's cruel hand,
A faith still waits, a quiet stand.

From ancient stones, the echoes rise,
Seek truth within the weary sighs.
In every tear that carves the night,
Hope flickers dim, yet shines so bright.

The lost, they wander, hearts in search,
Each path they tread, a sacred church.
In darkness' hold, the light is found,
In every prayer, new grace unbound.

The stars above, they tell the tale,
Of love that weaves through every veil.
Though anguished cries may pierce the sky,
In pain, God's mercy draws us nigh.

With every breath, we forge our way,
Through valleys low, to break of day.
In every heart, a gospel sings,
In life's abyss, redemption brings.

Messages from the Sanctuary of the Soul

Within the heart, a sacred space,
Where whispers dwell, in soft embrace.
Each thought a prayer, each sigh a hope,
In solitude, our spirits cope.

The sanctuary, calm and bright,
Illuminates the darkest night.
In quietude, we find our truth,
The wisdom borne from tender youth.

Messages wrapped in silence sweet,
Guiding the weary, sharing sweet.
Through trials faced, we seek the grace,
That rises softly in this place.

With each heartbeat, a story told,
In every moment, the spirit bold.
The soul's reflection, a mirror clear,
Reflecting love, dispelling fear.

From depths unknown, to heights untold,
The sanctuary, our hearts behold.
In whispered prayers, we find our role,
The messages speak from the soul.

Prayers Written in Tears

Each tear that falls, a silent plea,
A prayer that cleaves the darkened sea.
In sorrow's grip, our spirits bend,
Yet hope resides around the bend.

With trembling hands, we write our song,
In every loss, we still belong.
For every ache, a healing touch,
In every wound, love means so much.

The paper soaked in dreams once bright,
Now soaked in prayers, lost to the night.
Yet through the pain, we seek the dawn,
In tears, the strength to carry on.

The heavens listen, hearts in prayer,
Each whispered word, a breath we share.
Though clouds may gather, storms may rage,
In faith, we turn another page.

So let the tears flow like a stream,
In every drop, a sacred dream.
For through the sorrow, joy will bloom,
In prayers written, dispelling gloom.

The Saint's Silent Letters

In quiet moments, letters penned,
By saints who know, love will not end.
Their whispers drift on sacred air,
Silent witness, woven prayer.

With ink of faith, each line embraces,
The trials faced, the holy places.
In solitude, their truth unfolds,
In every letter, love retold.

Through trials fierce and valleys deep,
The saints embolden, never sleep.
Their silent words, like guiding stars,
Illuminate the path from scars.

Each letter speaks of grace in pain,
The strength to rise, again, again.
In every heart, a truth they share,
In every soul, their loving care.

So may we write with hearts afire,
In silent letters, our soul's desire.
In faith united, hand in hand,
We follow where the saints have stand.

The Lament of Inexpressible Thought

In the silence where shadows dwell,
Thoughts unspoken weave a spell,
Whispers of faith, lost in the night,
Yearning for solace, chasing the light.

Hearts ache, a song left unsung,
In the depths, where pain is flung,
The mind's burden, a sacred cry,
Yearning for grace, reaching the sky.

Through the darkness, a flicker appears,
In each moment, we face our fears,
With every pulse, a prayer we weave,
Resting in hope, we learn to believe.

In every tear, a story unfolds,
A tapestry woven with threads of gold,
Seek not for words, but feel the heart,
In the silence, creation's art.

So let us dwell in the quiet of thought,
Embrace the lesson that sorrow has taught,
For in our lament, we find the way,
To the dawn of a brighter day.

Sacred Dreams Unvoiced

In the twilight where dreams take flight,
Whispers of hope illuminate the night,
Silent visions, cloaked in grace,
Yearning for time and embrace.

These dreams, untouched by worldly eyes,
Dance in the hush, beneath the skies,
Bold aspirations, unspoken prayers,
Carried on wings, the spirit dares.

In the heart's chambers, a flame ignites,
Filled with longing, it softly writes,
Each heartbeat a hymn, a sacred call,
In the depths of silence, we rise, we fall.

With every breath, these dreams resound,
A cosmic melody, lost then found,
In the stillness, we chase what is real,
Daring to dream, daring to feel.

As dawn breaks, we venture anew,
Emboldened by dreams that we pursue,
For in the realm of the unvoiced,
Our spirits awaken, rejoice, rejoice.

Chronicles of the Heart's Solitude

In solitude, the heart finds peace,
Amidst the chaos, a sweet release,
Walls of silence, a sacred space,
Where love unfolds in a gentle embrace.

Through whispered prayers, the soul takes flight,
In quiet corners, it seeks the light,
Each tear a tale, each sigh a song,
In the stillness, we learn to belong.

Time stretches thin, yet vast it feels,
In the heart's realm, the spirit heals,
Pages turn in an unseen book,
Where faith ignites, and angels look.

Emotions dance in the absence of sound,
In the heart's solitude, wisdom is found,
Journey within, let the stillness flow,
In embrace of silence, we learn and grow.

So let us cherish this sacred space,
Where love's quiet whisper leaves a trace,
For in solitude, we find our worth,
A testament to our journey on Earth.

Divine Echoes of the Unsent

In letters penned but never sent,
An echo of love, forever pent,
In sacred ink, emotions bleed,
Words unsaid, like a whispered creed.

Each stroke a prayer, a fervent plea,
From trembling hands seeking to be free,
For in the void, the heart draws near,
To the divine, beyond all fear.

These echoes linger, soft and kind,
In the depths of the soul, forever entwined,
In unspoken thoughts, connections grow,
A tapestry of love, woven slow.

Time may fade, yet these echoes stay,
In the silence, they guide our way,
Carried on winds of sacred light,
Illuminating shadows, banishing night.

So let us treasure these words unvoiced,
In their stillness, our hearts rejoice,
For in the divine, we find our peace,
A chorus of love that shall never cease.

Psalms of the Unsung

In the shadowed halls of grace,
Whispers of the heart do race.
Unseen spirits guide the way,
In the silence, hope will stay.

Beneath the weight of sorrowed skies,
Faith like ashes softly lies.
Yet in quiet strength we find,
The light of love intertwined.

Voices lost in the night's embrace,
Songs of joy, we will retrace.
Through our trials, we shall rise,
Seeking truth that never dies.

With humble hearts, we bend our knees,
Offering prayers upon the breeze.
For every tear that fills the night,
A dawn shall break with brilliant light.

In hidden places, blessings bloom,
While the world seems shrouded in gloom.
Let us sing our praises loud,
For we are loved, forever proud.

Silent Cries to Heaven

In the stillness of the night,
Voices tremble, seeking light.
Silent pleas on whispered breath,
Yearning life, defying death.

Oh, the burden of the soul,
Grieving parts we can't control.
Each tear a prayer that finds its way,
To the heavens, where angels sway.

Lonely hearts seek divine embrace,
In their longing, they find grace.
Every struggle, every sigh,
Leads us closer to the sky.

Hope is but a fragile thread,
Woven with the words once said.
In the darkness, light we crave,
Let our spirits gently wave.

For in silence, truth resides,
In still waters, peace abides.
Toward the heavens, let us strive,
With each breath, we come alive.

The Testament of Loneliness

In the quiet of the mind,
Loneliness, a friend we find.
Echoes of a love once near,
Now just whispers, laced with fear.

Though the world can feel so vast,
In solitude, our shadows cast.
In the chambers of the heart,
We gather pieces, torn apart.

With every tear that stains the ground,
A testament in silence found.
Though we walk this path alone,
In the stillness, kindness grown.

Through the trials, we shall learn,
How the flame of hope can burn.
In our journey, strength abides,
As we cling to love that guides.

For the lonely, seek the light,
In the depths of darkest night.
With each sigh, a prayer takes flight,
In our hearts, the truth ignites.

Messages for the Unseen

In the dusk where shadows play,
Messages for souls at bay.
Through the mist, a gentle call,
In the silence, we stand tall.

Whispers linger in the air,
Carried forth on wings of prayer.
To the unseen, we send our love,
Like a prayer that soars above.

In our dreams, we meet again,
Bound by faith, beyond the pain.
With each step, we find a way,
To embrace the dawn of day.

Threads of fate that intertwine,
Binding hearts through space and time.
In every tear, a sacred bond,
Uniting us with love's great dawn.

As the stars begin to gleam,
We remember every dream.
For the unseen, we shall strive,
In our hearts, love stays alive.

Heavenly Messages Entwined in Silence

In the quiet of the night, we listen,
Whispers dance on the breath of prayer.
Angels weave their tales in shadows,
Hearts alight with a sacred flare.

Stars adorn the velvet sky,
Each a beacon of hope and grace.
In the stillness, spirits arise,
Guiding souls to a holy place.

Light descends like morning dew,
Blessings flow from the Divine.
In silence, all wonders bloom,
A tapestry of love entwined.

Through valleys of doubt, we wander,
Yet faith carries the weight of years.
In the silence of our longings,
God's embrace wipes away our tears.

Heaven's messages, soft and clear,
Speak of truth beyond our sight.
In the hush of our humble hearts,
Eternal hope ignites the night.

The Echo of Intentions

In every thought, a prayer is born,
Ripples echo through the vast expanse.
Waves of kindness softly drawn,
Turning fate with sacred chance.

Intentions pure as morning light,
Shift the shadows, mend the seams.
In the depths, we find our fight,
Guided by our truest dreams.

Each heartbeat sings a holy song,
Carried forth on winds of grace.
In the moments we belong,
We find ourselves in love's embrace.

As the world spins ever round,
Love transcends the passing time.
In every soul, a spark is found,
Lighting paths with sacred rhyme.

The echoes linger in the still,
Reminders of what we can be.
With every breath, we choose to fill,
The universe with harmony.

Invisible Ink, Visible Yearning

Words unspoken ink the air,
Yearnings float like drifting leaves.
In the silence, honest prayer,
The heart unfolds, the spirit weaves.

Beneath the surface, truth resides,
Hidden deep in every glance.
Love's narrative forever hides,
Awaiting the chance to advance.

Each unwritten word a sigh,
A testament to the divine.
In our longing, we defy,
The boundaries of space and time.

Hope, a whisper on the breeze,
Binds our souls in tender hands.
With every pulse, we seek to seize,
The silent call that understands.

Invisible ink tattooed in light,
Visible yearning fuels the flame.
In the deep, our spirits ignite,
Each moment speaks a sacred name.

Psalters of the Unshared

In the garden, secrets bloom,
Psalters sung in quiet tones.
Each petal carries whispered rooms,
Where love emerges from the stones.

Beneath the sun's embracing gaze,
Unfolding stories of the heart.
In every shadow, light will blaze,
Uniting souls that remain apart.

Voices soar on winds of prayer,
Gentle hymns woven as one.
Bound by faith, they lift the air,
In the tapestry of the undone.

Every tear, a song unshared,
A melody of longing's quest.
In the silence, all are bared,
Seeking solace, finding rest.

Psalters echo through the night,
Reminders of the love we seek.
In the darkness, there is light,
A promise whispered soft and sweet.

Sacrificial Prayers for the Unheard

In whispers low, we call your name,
With hearts aflame, we feel the same.
These prayers rise, like incense sweet,
For all those souls who feel defeat.

We cast our hopes upon the sky,
Where silent ones, their echoes sigh.
In shadows cast, their pain we bear,
A sacred bond, a holy prayer.

The tears of many flow as one,
Beneath the veil, till day is done.
With open hands, we seek the grace,
To touch the stars, to find our place.

Through night's embrace, we seek the light,
In quiet trust, we find our fight.
The unheard voices rise and blend,
A chorus strong, until the end.

So let us stand where few will tread,
And hold the weight of words unsaid.
In sacrificial love, we pray,
For all the lost, to find their way.

The Quietude of Missed Connections

In stillness deep, the heart aligns,
With silent hopes, the spirit shines.
Each glance a story, left untold,
A warmth unique, in echoes bold.

The paths we cross, like fleeting dreams,
In gentle whispers, life redeems.
A brush of hands, a fleeting chance,
In quietude, our souls advance.

Yet, missed the beat that time has spun,
A melody, forever run.
In shadows cast, we linger still,
As silent prayers fulfill the will.

Through every pause, a lesson learned,
Each moment lost, for which we yearned.
In sacred spaces, dreams collide,
Where hope abounds, and hearts confide.

Though missed connections leave a hole,
In silence found, we seek the whole.
With open hearts, we forge ahead,
In quietude, our spirits fed.

Transcendent Sentiments in Invisibility

Beneath the veil of everyday,
Our souls entwined, in soft array.
Invisibility, a sacred guise,
Where spirit soars, beyond the eyes.

We roam the paths, both near and far,
In unseen worlds, we find our star.
Transcendent dreams in shadows play,
A dance of light on night's display.

For those who dwell in hidden grace,
Their radiant hearts, time can't erase.
In silence strong, their truths emerge,
Through whispered prayers, our hopes converge.

Though often lost to worldly sight,
Their love ignites the deepest light.
Invisibility, a holy crown,
Where sacred souls will never drown.

So let us seek the unseen wise,
And cherish love, despite the skies.
Transcendent joys in quiet lands,
Through invisible threads, our hearts expand.

Parables of the Unsung

In stories told, without a sound,
The unsung heroes, lost but found.
With every step, their truths bestow,
A legacy in hearts that glow.

Through trials faced, their voices rise,
In humble frames, the spirit flies.
Parables woven in the night,
Illuminate with inner light.

They labor hard, their struggles bare,
In quiet grace, they find their prayer.
For every deed the world forgets,
In silent strength, the heart connects.

So let us honor all they've given,
Through every path their lives have riven.
In every tale of love and fight,
The unsung stand, a beacon bright.

With open arms, we share their song,
In unity, where we belong.
Parables of love that never cease,
In silent hearts, we find our peace.

Digital Prayers in the Void

In the glow of screens we pray,
Whispers lost in the light of day.
Fingers dance on keys so cold,
Seeking solace, secrets unfold.

Silent echoes through the cloud,
Voices muffled, yet so loud.
In the data stream we yearn,
For a kindness, a heart to turn.

Pixels gather like grains of sand,
Each desire a fragile strand.
In this realm where shadows blend,
We find hope, our spirits mend.

Connections forged in wires thin,
Breathing life through where we've been.
Let our prayers rise and soar,
Through the void, forevermore.

Together we light the night,
With digital candles burning bright.
In shared silence, we unite,
And find peace in the virtual light.

Litany for the Lost Words

Lost in the echoes of the past,
Words unspoken, shadows cast.
In the silence, we implore,
Bring back voices, let them soar.

Streets once filled with laughter's sound,
Now a hush, no joy found.
Every whisper turned to dust,
In these moments, we still trust.

Gathered thoughts upon the breeze,
Seeking truth with gentle ease.
With each breath, we pray for grace,
To find meaning in this space.

Oh, the stories left untold,
Where they wander, growing old.
In the night, we search and seek,
Words that heal the heart's mystique.

From the depths, we raise our voice,
In lost words, we make our choice.
A litany for all we crave,
In the silence, let us save.

Grails of Unsent Maledictions

In the shadows where they dwell,
Grails of pain, a haunting spell.
Silent screams, yet unexpressed,
In our hearts, they find no rest.

Held within this heavy chest,
Maledictions we can't contest.
Wishing peace but feeling strife,
Battling demons with this life.

For every wound we carry tight,
A yearning for the sacred light.
In our sorrow, we shall find,
The strength to leave the dark behind.

Through the storms, our spirits clash,
In the quiet, a sacred flash.
Forgive the words we'd never share,
In the void, lift up a prayer.

Grails of sorrow turn to gold,
In our hearts, stories unfold.
From each wound, a lesson grows,
In the silence, love still flows.

Threads of Faith Unwoven

Threads of faith, frayed and torn,
In the night, a soul reborn.
Weaving dreams from mortal strife,
Sewing hope into this life.

Each stitch a prayer, each knot a test,
In the tapestry, we find rest.
Vows once spoken, tangled tight,
Fading slowly from our sight.

In the silence, doubts reside,
Yet in hearts, the truth abides.
Unraveling doubts, we press on,
Trusting light before the dawn.

With every fiber, tales we spin,
Through life's weave, we seek within.
Even when the threads unwind,
Faith remains, forever kind.

With gentle hands, we mend the seams,
Stitching love back into dreams.
In the end, the fabric whole,
Threads of faith embrace the soul.

The Edict of Silent Supplications

In the hush of twilight's grace,
Hearts are drawn to sacred space.
Beneath the stars, they lift their pleas,
To the One who hears, the One who sees.

With whispers soft, faith intertwines,
Hope blooms bright, like sacred vines.
Each drop of tear an act of trust,
In His love, we find our must.

Voices blend in quiet prayer,
Angels gather, wisdom share.
In the silence, burdens cease,
As souls embrace the gift of peace.

Through shadows deep, light breaks anew,
Guiding hearts to what is true.
Ears attuned to His soft call,
In unity, we rise, we fall.

So let the echoes softly sing,
Of hope restored, of faith's offering.
For in these silent supplications,
Dwells the heart of all creations.

Whispers of the Soul's Yearning

In the quiet of dawn's embrace,
The soul reveals its hidden face.
Yearning voices, drawn to the light,
Seek the truth through endless night.

Like rivers flowing towards the sea,
Each heart craves its destiny.
In moments hushed, they seek to find,
The gentle pull of the divine.

With every breath, a sacred sigh,
Beneath the vast and open sky.
Whispers dance on softest air,
A symphony of earnest prayer.

The soul ascends on wings unseen,
In every struggle lies the dream.
For deep within, the flame ignites,
As love's pure strength in darkness fights.

So heed the calls that softly blend,
Each yearning soul, a tale to send.
In whispers, truths begin to gleam,
A united chorus, a shared dream.

Ashes of What Could Have Been

In the remnants of the past we see,
Ashes linger where dreams used to be.
Memories fade like autumn leaves,
But hope remains, though time deceives.

What could have been, in shadows tread,
Lost in silence, the words left unsaid.
Yet from the ash, the spirit blooms,
In every heart, a flower assumes.

Through trials faced and battles won,
A testament to what's begun.
From loss we rise, our souls aligned,
In the embers, new paths we find.

The past, a canvas painted gray,
Still teaches us, day by day.
From every scar, a lesson grows,
In sorrow's depths, true wisdom flows.

So let the ashes be our guide,
In every tear, we've not denied.
For what could have been, still finds its place,
In the sacred dance of time and grace.

The Untold Testament of the Spirit

In the depth of quiet nights we stand,
Seeking wisdom, hand in hand.
An untold tale of soul and fate,
Whispers of love that resonate.

In the shadows, truth unfolds,
A righteous path for hearts so bold.
Each spirit carries ancient lore,
Of journeys taken, and much more.

From the valley low to mountains high,
In faith's embrace, we soar, we fly.
Every breath, a sacred chant,
The spirit's song, forever haunts.

Through trials faced, we find our worth,
A testament of rebirth.
For in each struggle, light is born,
A shining path through nights forlorn.

So let the gospel of the heart
Guide us forth, a sacred art.
In every soul, a truth to glean,
The untold testament, serene.

Untamed Confessions

In shadows cast by doubt's fierce hand,
I seek the light that leads to land.
Each breath a prayer, each sigh a plea,
Untamed confessions, I long to be free.

With whispers that echo in the night,
I wrestle with fears that shun the light.
In every battle, a truth I find,
An untamed spirit, forever unconfined.

Sacred tears fall to the ground,
In the stillness, a grace is found.
Forgive me, Lord, for my wandering ways,
In my confessions, I give You praise.

As dawn unveils a fresh new day,
I lay my burdens; they fade away.
In the chorus of life, I long to sing,
My untamed heart to You I bring.

Bless these confessions, humble and true,
May they guide me closer, ever anew.
In the whispers of faith, I now abide,
With untamed confessions, forever my guide.

Unvoiced Sermons of the Soul

In silence deep, my spirit speaks,
Unvoiced sermons, wisdom seeks.
Within the stillness, a message flows,
The heart's true story, the world bestows.

With every heartbeat, a lesson learned,
In shadows of doubt, faith is burned.
In the quiet grace, I find my way,
Unvoiced, yet loud, the soul's ballet.

I walk a path unseen, unknown,
In the depths, my faith has grown.
With every breath, divinity calls,
In unvoiced sermons, love enthralls.

The soul's reflection, a sacred art,
In solitude, I am set apart.
With hushed revelations, my spirit plays,
In unvoiced sermons, I find my gaze.

A testament to the divine embrace,
In stillness, my heart finds its place.
For in silence, the truth breaks through,
Unvoiced sermons, a gift to pursue.

Scrolls of Unexpressed Yearning

In the quiet night, I write my heart,
Scrolls of yearning, a sacred art.
Each line a wish, unpressed by time,
In whispered prayers, I seek to climb.

With ink of faith, I etch my dreams,
In the stillness, the spirit gleams.
Longing for grace, I pen my truth,
In unexpressed words, lies my youth.

With every stroke, my soul takes flight,
In the tapestry woven, day and night.
Scrolls of yearning held close to me,
In sacred silence, my heart is free.

A longing deep, a sacred fire,
To write of love, to aspire.
In the margins, hope gently spreads,
Scrolls of yearning in silent threads.

With every verse, a promise flows,
Through unexpressed yearning, vision grows.
In the pages of faith, I find my call,
Scrolls of yearning, uniting us all.

The Sanctuary of Unshared Reflections

In the sanctuary, I seek retreat,
Where whispers echo, and stillness meets.
Unshared reflections, a sacred place,
In the quiet, I find Your grace.

With every thought, a prayer ascends,
In silent dialogue, my spirit mends.
Among the shadows, light gently weaves,
Unshared reflections, my heart believes.

In sacred moments, I hold my breath,
In the sanctuary, there's life in death.
With unspoken burdens, I lay them bare,
In the stillness, I find You there.

With every heartbeat, a promise sworn,
In the sanctuary, my soul reborn.
Unshared reflections, a treasure deep,
In silent devotion, my spirit keeps.

From the depths of silence, a song I sing,
In the sanctuary, my heart takes wing.
With unshared reflections, I rise anew,
In the quiet embrace, I return to You.

Hushed Benedictions

In the quiet of the morn, we pray,
Whispers of gratitude softly sway.
Hearts entwined in sacred grace,
Finding solace in this holy space.

Each breath a blessing, pure and bright,
Guided by the gentle light.
In silence, we seek the divine,
A tapestry of love we bind.

The angels' wings brush past our soul,
Embracing us, making us whole.
With every tear, a seed is sown,
In faith, we find our way back home.

Together we lift our voices high,
United in spirit, we soar the sky.
Hushed benedictions fill the air,
In this moment, nothing can compare.

In the twilight hour, when stillness reigns,
We offer our hearts, releasing our chains.
With fervent hope and poised intent,
We rise, a chorus, heaven sent.

Reverent Thoughts in Twilight

As daylight fades, we gather near,
Wrapped in warmth, casting off fear.
With reverent thoughts, we ponder deep,
In twilight's embrace, our spirits leap.

The stars awake, like candles bright,
Illuminating the coming night.
Each shimmer a promise from above,
A radiant echo of endless love.

In these moments, so tender and clear,
Whispers of wisdom softly appear.
We reflect on paths we've walked anew,
In every shadow, the divine shines through.

With one heartbeat, we seek to connect,
In the silence, we earn our respect.
With humble hearts and open hands,
We dance to the tune that grace commands.

The veil grows thin, the world grows still,
In the depths of night, our spirits fill.
With reverent thoughts, we find our peace,
In this sacred moment, we are released.

Chants of the Untold

From deep within, a chant arises,
A melody of truth, no disguises.
Voices weave through sacred air,
Tales of love, of hope, and prayer.

Ancient hymns echo in our soul,
Guiding us, making us whole.
In the stillness, we find our way,
Chants of the untold, here to stay.

Through trials faced and battles won,
We sing for those, the lost, the shunned.
Each note a reminder, we are one,
A symphony beneath the sun.

In every heart, a story lies,
A testament to how we rise.
With every chant, we break our mold,
In unity, our strength unfolds.

So let us gather, let voices blend,
A sacred promise, we transcend.
In the tapestry of life retold,
We find our purpose through chants of old.

Dialogues with the Divine

In the still of night, we whisper low,
Seeking answers, yearning to know.
Each dialogue, a sacred thread,
Connecting us to what lies ahead.

With open hearts, we question fate,
As stars align, we contemplate.
In every silence, a voice we hear,
Dialogues with the divine draw near.

Through trials faced, we seek the light,
In every struggle, there's wisdom bright.
An unseen hand, we feel so close,
In this exchange, love overflows.

As dawn breaks, we greet anew,
With grace-filled hearts, we make our due.
In every moment, we find the sign,
In these dialogues, the spirit's line.

So lift your gaze, let courage swell,
In quietude, we hear the spell.
Each question answered, a promise divine,
Together we journey, forever intertwined.

Hymns of the Unexpressed

In shadows deep, where whispers dwell,
A sacred space, a silent bell.
Hearts entwined in prayerful breath,
Finding light in stillness, rest.

Voices rise in inward song,
Where broken souls to One belong.
In humble grace, we seek to find,
The love that binds all heart and mind.

The shimmering stars, His gentle art,
Each twinkle a hope, a brand new start.
With open palms, our spirits soar,
In the quiet night, we seek Him more.

Bound by faith, our worries cease,
In surrender, we find our peace.
The road may twist, the path may turn,
Yet in our hearts, His flame will burn.

Together in this holy space,
We lift our hands in warm embrace.
Through trials faced, our spirits climb,
In hymns of love, transcending time.

Chronicles of Silent Devotion

In the stillness, the soul abides,
In whispered prayers, our hope resides.
With every sigh, a story told,
Of love divine, eternal, bold.

Beneath the stars, our dreams we lay,
In shadows cast, we find our way.
Each heartbeat echoes sacred lore,
In silence deep, we long for more.

The morning sun, a gentle call,
To rise anew, to break the fall.
With steadfast faith, we journey on,
In quiet strength, our fears are gone.

Every tear, a sacred thread,
Woven in grace, where angels tread.
In moments hushed, we journey near,
To feel His love, to cast off fear.

A testament of hearts ablaze,
In the quiet, we sing His praise.
Though words may fade, devotion stays,
In chronicles of silent days.

The Unsent Scrolls of the Soul

Unfold the scrolls, the heart's design,
Crafted in love, by hands divine.
With ink of faith, in shadows cast,
The echoes of the future and past.

In absence felt, His presence swells,
A sacred truth, the spirit tells.
With every breath, we weave the thread,
Connecting souls, where angels tread.

The quiet nights, a canvas bright,
Stars paint the dreams, embroider light.
Each moment holds a tender grace,
As silence wraps us in His embrace.

In unspoken words, we find release,
In loving stillness, a perfect peace.
Though letters fade, the feelings stay,
The unexpressed within the fray.

Together in this sacred place,
We ponder love, we seek His face.
Though unsent, these scrolls hold the key,
To unlock grace, and set us free.

Divine Soliloquy in Stillness

In serene whispers, thoughts unite,
Where silence breathes, we find the light.
Across the void, a gentle plea,
In devotion's glow, we long to be.

Each fleeting moment, soft and true,
The heart's refrain, a sacred view.
In stillness deep, we shed our tears,
Embracing love that calms our fears.

Time stands still, the world may spin,
Yet in this space, our truth begins.
With silent prayers, our spirits rise,
In heavenly peace, beneath the skies.

The echo lingers, a soothing balm,
In hushed supplications, find our calm.
Through vibrant thoughts, whispers take flight,
In divine soliloquy, pure delight.

Together we tread this path of grace,
In stillness found, our sacred space.
As hearts align, we magnify,
The love that dwells, the reason why.

Ciphers of the Heart

In whispering winds, the spirits sigh,
Secrets of love, the soul's soft cry.
Guided by stars, we seek the light,
In shadows deep, faith takes its flight.

Each tear fallen, a prayer in disguise,
Painting the path, where hope often lies.
Wrapped in grace, our hearts uncoil,
In silence, we tread, through sacred soil.

With burdens shared, the burdens cease,
In community, we find our peace.
Voices combining, a sacred song,
In unity, we have belonged.

Open your heart to the gentle breeze,
Let it carry away your unease.
For in the ciphers, wisdom is found,
In love's embrace, all are unbound.

So linger awhile in the hush of night,
Where echoes of faith glow ever bright.
Hold fast to dreams on this sacred art,
For here lies the truth—ciphers of the heart.

Unuttered Tenets

Words unspoken, yet profoundly felt,
In the quiet whir, our fates are dealt.
Whispers of truth that softly gleam,
In the silence, we dare to dream.

Every heartbeat, a sacred creed,
Nurtured by love, our fundamental need.
In the stillness, our spirits soar,
Opening pathways to the evermore.

Ancient lessons bloom anew,
In the void, faith is our view.
Unuttered tenets, profound and wise,
Guide us hidden, where the heart lies.

In seeking solace, we find our home,
Through uncharted skies, we freely roam.
For in each glance, a universe waits,
Unuttered truths unlock the gates.

So gather the whispers, embrace the night,
Know in your heart, all can be right.
With unuttered tenets, we go forth,
To illuminate the unseen worth.

Silent Chronicles of Faith

In the stillness of dawn, the shadows play,
Silent chronicles whisper and sway.
In every heartbeat, a story unfolds,
Of trials endured and of courage untold.

Tracing the lines etched in time,
Moments cherished, both bitter and sublime.
Faith written softly on the canvas of skies,
Drawing us closer as our spirits rise.

In solitude's embrace, we find our guide,
With each breath, the soul opens wide.
Through silent worlds, our spirits ignite,
Casting aside the shrouds of night.

The echoes of prayer weave through the trees,
Carried on winds with elegant ease.
And in the quiet, our hearts align,
Sharing the sacred, the divine design.

Join the dance of the hushed, serene,
Where hope and love reign evergreen.
For in silent chronicles, we are reborn,
In the arms of faith, each new dawn.

The Book of What Could Be

Turn the pages of what might arise,
In the realm of dreams, endless skies.
With faith as ink, our destinies flow,
In the book of what could be, let love grow.

Each chapter written with threads of light,
Bearing witness to trials and plight.
Weaves of hope stitch the seams of fate,
In the hands of grace, we navigate.

What if the dawn breaks with newfound eyes?
What if the heart learns to recognize?
In the uncharted, courage takes flight,
Choosing the path that turns darkness bright.

Hold fast the vision, the dreams we share,
In unity's might, together we care.
For the book is open, its narrative free,
Guided by love, we'll write what could be.

So gather your dreams, let them take flight,
In the book of what could be, every soul ignites.
With faith as our compass, our spirits set free,
Together we'll pen our sweet destiny.

Sacred Notes to the Silence

In stillness lies a whispered grace,
Each breath a prayer in this holy place.
Above the noise, a soft refrain,
Echoes of love, free from pain.

Candles flicker with sacred light,
Guiding souls through the tranquil night.
In shadows deep, the spirit sings,
A harmony of divine things.

Each tear a testament of care,
In silence, we find answers rare.
Hearts entwined in fragile peace,
In quiet faith, our worries cease.

Through the silence, we seek the dawn,
When hope arises, fears withdrawn.
With every note, a story told,
Of love eternal, brave and bold.

In sacred silence, together we stand,
With open hearts, a unified band.
In the hush, our souls take flight,
To sing the praises of the Light.

Prayers of the Untold

Within the depths of aching souls,
Lie prayers unspoken, vivid scrolls.
In shadows cast by doubt and fear,
Lies a longing for the One who's near.

Each heartbeat echoes a silent plea,
For strength, for grace, for chance to be.
In every sigh, a whisper of hope,
Through trials faced, we learn to cope.

Beneath the weight of unseen scars,
Resilience blooms like distant stars.
In whispered prayers, we find our fate,
In love's embrace, we navigate.

With palms uplifted, in humble trust,
We seek the Light, as all hearts must.
Each prayer a wave, towards the shore,
Where faith and love forever soar.

In the tapestry of souls combined,
Lie stories of grace and paths aligned.
Together we rise, together we stand,
In prayers of the untold, hand in hand.

Reverent Ink of the Heart

With every stroke of pen on page,
The heart unveils its sacred sage.
In ink that flows like rivers deep,
We write the truths we hold and keep.

Each word a testament of grace,
In reverence, we find our place.
Stories written in silent tears,
Transforming pain into the years.

With gentle hands, we craft the light,
As darkness fades, revealing sight.
In verses spun of love's embrace,
We honor every sacred space.

Through trials faced and burdens shared,
Ink becomes the balm we dared.
Every line a bridge we build,
To connect what love fulfilled.

In reverent ink, our souls take flight,
Transforming shadows into light.
Together, we weave a tapestry bright,
With every heartbeat, find the rite.

Celestial Compositions Unshared

In the quiet night, compositions dwell,
Songs of the stars, their secrets to tell.
Each twinkle cast in the sky above,
A melody woven of faith and love.

With every hush of the evening breeze,
Whispers of angels, a gentle tease.
In the cosmos, our dreams collide,
As celestial bodies in grace abide.

We gather moments, precious and bright,
In the fabric of dreams, a wondrous sight.
Each heartbeat aligns in whispers unheard,
An orchestra played, each note a word.

Though unshared, this song still sings,
In the heart's depths, where pure joy clings.
With every breath, we join the dance,
In these celestial realms, we take our chance.

United we stand, though worlds apart,
In compositions grand, we play our part.
Underneath the vast and starlit spree,
We are together, eternally free.

The Sacred Silence of Unwritten Thoughts

In the hush of night, dreams take flight,
Floating softly, bathed in light.
Unseen prayers whispered in the dark,
Echoes linger like a sacred spark.

Hearts in shadows, seeking peace,
Thoughts like rivers, flow and cease.
In silence, wisdom softly dwells,
A well of grace where spirit swells.

Every sigh a humble plea,
To the stars, infinity.
In the stillness, truth unveils,
The softest sound, the heart's own gales.

Words unspoken, heavy yet light,
Carried forth on wings of night.
Holding secrets of the soul,
In the quiet, we are whole.

Timeless moments, divine embrace,
Lost in the vast, eternal space.
In this silence, we unite,
In sacred whispers, pure delight.

The Ascendant Yearning

Awakening spirit, a distant call,
Yearning for the rise, to break the fall.
With every heartbeat, hope ignites,
A flame ascending, reaching heights.

In the valley of solitude, we strive,
Through shadows deep, our dreams revive.
A path uncertain, yet we tread,
Finding solace where angels tread.

Hands raised high to the endless sky,
In this moment, we're free to fly.
With faith as our guide, we overcome,
In the light of love, we become one.

Every challenge, a stepping stone,
In unity, we are never alone.
Resolute hearts, never to yield,
In the battle, our strength revealed.

With voices lifted, we sing of grace,
Filling the void of time and space.
In the chorus of hope, we align,
In the garden of dreams, we entwine.

Celestial Whispers Unheard

Stars align in the heavenly dome,
Silent whispers call us home.
In the stillness of twilight's reign,
Hearts awaken, shedding pain.

Each breath a prayer, unvoiced yet clear,
Echoing love that draws us near.
In the quiet, a promise waits,
Boundless grace that resonates.

Through the veils of time, we seek,
Light eternal, strong yet meek.
Voices murmur in graceful flight,
Guiding us through the depths of night.

In the silence, truth will grow,
Seeds of faith in our hearts sow.
With every heartbeat, divine embrace,
In the whispers, we find our place.

Celestial echoes bloom in the dark,
Illuminating each hidden spark.
In the quiet, we learn to see,
The sacred bond, you and me.

Soft Echoes in the Temple of Silence

In the temple where silence reigns,
Soft echoes dance, breaking chains.
Threads of stillness weave and twine,
A sacred space where spirits shine.

With gentle hands, we seek to feel,
The beauty in quiet, a sacred seal.
All thoughts suspended, time a mist,
In whispers sweet, we coexist.

Each heartbeat's rhythm, a sacred song,
In contemplation, we find where we belong.
The pulse of life, a sacred hymn,
In the dark, the light grows dim.

In unity, we gather near,
Voices soft as the evening clear.
With every breath, we find the grace,
In the silence, we embrace.

In the echoes of the heart's own peace,
The temple echoes, troubles cease.
In silent reverence, we align,
In the sacred still, we define.

Wisdom of Unspoken Gratitude

In silence, hearts entwine with grace,
A gentle breath, in love's embrace.
Each moment cherished, a sacred thread,
In whispered thanks, our spirits wed.

The dawn unfolds, a canvas bright,
Soft rays of warmth, dispelling night.
Through humble hearts, the blessings flow,
In silent prayers, our spirits grow.

Nature hums a sacred tune,
The fluttering leaves beneath the moon.
In every sigh, a story told,
Of gratitude, both shy and bold.

In quietude, we find our song,
Where shadows dwell, and we belong.
The beauty lies in what we feel,
Unspoken love, our souls reveal.

So let us walk with open eyes,
In every laugh, in every sigh.
With each heartbeat, let us know,
The gift of grace in ebb and flow.

Celestial Correspondence in Stillness

In the stillness of the night sky,
Stars converse, they wink and sigh.
A cosmic dance, they twinkle bright,
In silence, they share divine light.

Beneath the vast and endless dome,
We seek connection, we feel at home.
Whispers of wisdom, gentle and clear,
Guiding our souls, dispelling fear.

The moon, a keeper of our dreams,
Reflects our hopes, the softest beams.
In twilight hours, the spirits play,
In each heartbeat, they find their way.

Celestial echoes of love's decree,
Remind us of our unity.
In the hush of night, we hear the call,
The universe, a friend to all.

In sacred stillness, let us dwell,
Embracing all, both heaven and hell.
In every breath, a promise made,
In cosmic arms, our fears allayed.

Whispers of the Unwritten

In margins where the silence hums,
The beauty of the unwritten comes.
Each thought a seed, in shadows cast,
Awaiting light, to bloom at last.

The pages wait, their tales untold,
In every sigh, a life unfolds.
In whispers soft, the truth we find,
With gentle hands, we shape the mind.

The pen may pause, but hearts still speak,
In every tear, in every peak.
The stories linger, in dreams they lie,
A testament to all we try.

In stillness deep, our spirits yearn,
With every turn, another burn.
On fragile sheets, we leave our trace,
In unmarked paths, we find our place.

So let us voice the quiet song,
In words unformed, we all belong.
The unwritten whispers of our quest,
In every heart, a sacred rest.

Divine Scribbles in the Void

Amidst the void, where silence reigns,
Divine scribbles, in ethereal chains.
Each mark a spark, a thought divine,
In cosmic dreams, our fates align.

The empty space, a canvas fair,
Invites our hopes, invites our prayer.
In fragments lost, the truth emerges,
In every line, a spirit surges.

Glimmers of light, a fleeting grace,
In void we search, we find our place.
The scribbles tell of love unfurled,
A map to guide, through this vast world.

With every stroke, creation breathes,
In silent moments, the heart believes.
In divine chaos, our souls take flight,
Finding solace in the night.

So let us dance in realms unseen,
With scribbles bold and hearts serene.
In every void, a sacred trace,
Reflecting love, embracing grace.

Offerings in Ink

In shadows cast by candle light,
We pen our hopes, our souls in flight.
Each written word, an offering rare,
Laid down in prayer, light as air.

The ink runs deep, our hearts exposed,
In sacred texts, our faith is closed.
With every stroke, a promise made,
In whispers soft, our fears allayed.

The scribes of old, in silence knew,
The power held in every hue.
With every line, a bridge is formed,
Through trials faced, our spirits warmed.

A testament of love and grace,
In every curve, a sacred space.
We gather here with hearts entwined,
In ink we find what's left behind.

So let the pages come alive,
In offerings where dreams arrive.
With each reflection, we aspire,
To reach the heights, our souls afire.

Sacred Ink

With quill in hand, we trace the sky,
A testament of faith, we sigh.
The sacred ink, like blood divine,
In every vein, the light does shine.

Eternal truths on parchment laid,
In every word, the fears displayed.
We seek the path to wisdom's door,
In solemn thoughts, our spirits soar.

The scribes of ages, spirits bright,
They penned the world in darkest night.
With every letter, hearts entwined,
In sacred space, our lives defined.

Through trials faced, we draw the line,
With ink of hope, our hearts align.
In every stroke, a silent vow,
To cherish grace, to honor now.

A symphony of words that dance,
In holy spaces, we find our chance.
In every droplet, faith does flow,
With sacred ink, our spirits grow.

Silent Pages

In volumes deep, the silence speaks,
A language pure, for those who seek.
The pages turn with gentle grace,
Embracing all, a warm embrace.

Within the lines, the echoes chime,
A melody that transcends time.
In whispered hope, we find our way,
Through silent pages, night and day.

The heart finds rest in working words,
A song of truth, like song of birds.
In every space, a moment shines,
In silent pages, love entwines.

With every glance, a prayer is shared,
In quietude, our souls are bared.
A journey through the written art,
In silent pages, we find our heart.

As ink flows forth, a river wide,
In silent pages, we abide.
With humility, our spirits rise,
In written word, we touch the skies.

Reveries to the Celestial

In starry nights, we turn our gaze,
To realms beyond, where silence plays.
In reverie, we find our kin,
In whispered dreams, the light shines in.

With eyes closed tight, we seek the divine,
In cosmic dance, our souls align.
In every heartbeat, echoes sing,
To realms of light, our spirits cling.

The heavens call, a gentle plea,
In celestial songs, we long to be.
Through astral winds, our thoughts take flight,
In reveries, we touch the light.

In unison, our hearts awake,
To seek the truth in every shake.
With faith as guide, we journey far,
In reveries, we reach the star.

So let us dream, with open hearts,
In cosmic realms, our journey starts.
With every whisper, we are free,
In reveries to eternity.

Echoes of the Divine

In whispered tones, the spirit speaks,
Through ancient paths, the heart still seeks.
Echoes of grace in every breath,
A testament to life and death.

In every moment, sacred sound,
In silence deep, the truth is found.
Through gentle waves, the ripples flow,
In echoes, seeds of love we sow.

With hands outstretched to skies above,
We yearn for peace, we yearn for love.
The echoes ring, a lullaby,
In every note, we learn to fly.

Through trials faced, the heart does grow,
In every struggle, strength we show.
With echoes wild, we find our way,
To dance with light, to face the day.

So let the echoes guide our flight,
In every shadow, search for light.
With hearts ablaze, we now align,
In every breath, we hear the divine.

Divine Messages Unheard

In shadows deep, the spirit speaks,
A gentle touch, as silence peaks.
A path of light, though often veiled,
In heart's embrace, the truth unveiled.

When whispers soft beckon the soul,
To seek the grace that makes us whole.
In quietude, the answers lie,
Unseen by most, yet ever nigh.

Through trials faced, we learn to bend,
Each tear a sign, a message penned.
Divine intention flows like streams,
Transforming pain into our dreams.

For every doubt that clouds the mind,
A sacred truth we seek to find.
In prayerful hearts, the echoes rise,
A chorus heard beyond the skies.

So listen close, when stillness reigns,
The sacred whispers ease the pains.
With open hearts, let love abide,
In divine messages, we confide.

Sacred Whispers in the Silence

In twilight's hush, the spirit sighs,
With every breath, a soft reprise.
The cosmos hums a timeless tune,
Beneath the stars, the heart's monsoon.

Each moment still, the world fades out,
Where whispers dwell and fears devout.
In boundaryless grace, we meet,
The sacred pulse, our hearts' heartbeat.

For in the void, where shadows play,
A light emerges, guiding the way.
Through veils of doubt, we journey forth,
To find the source, the sacred worth.

The silence holds a promise clear,
In every prayer, our souls draw near.
With faith as wings, we soar and glide,
On sacred whispers, love our guide.

So let us gather 'round the flame,
In whispered truths, call His name.
For every heart that seeks to find,
In sacred silence, peace entwined.

Epistles of the Heart

With every beat, the heart composes,
Letters of love, like blooming roses.
Each handwritten note, a silent prayer,
In fleeting breath, we find Him there.

In every sorrow, joy is sewn,
Epistles written, seeds of grace grown.
Through trials faced, the lessons learned,
A tapestry of hearts discerned.

With ink of faith, we write our song,
In unison with the Divine throng.
On parchment soft, where shadows part,
The sacred words dwell in the heart.

To all who seek the voice of peace,
In every tear, a spark can cease.
Each epistle shared, our stories blend,
In love's embrace, we find our end.

So let your spirit take its flight,
With every letter, hearts ignite.
The epistles sing of love's embrace,
In every rhythm, we find grace.

Notes to the Eternal

In quiet moments, thoughts arise,
Notes to the Eternal in soft replies.
Each whisper penned on pages bare,
A testament of love laid bare.

Through swirling winds and endless skies,
The heart writes forth, with no disguise.
In every challenge, wisdom's muse,
Life's sacred lessons we must choose.

From depths of faith where shadows creep,
Our notes emerge, the soul's heartbeat.
In unity with the Divine source,
We trace the path of love's discourse.

With every pen, the spirit frees,
Crafting messages upon the breeze.
To those who listen, truth will sing,
In notes to the Eternal, hope we bring.

So write we shall, with fervent flame,
In gratitude, we call His name.
For every note, a sacred thread,
In the tapestry of love, we're led.

Psalms of the Unspoken

In the silence, whispers rise,
Hearts lifted towards the skies.
Seeking solace in the night,
Faint echoes of the Divine light.

Winds carry the words once lost,
Faithful souls, no matter the cost.
In the shadows they softly tread,
Nurtured by the hope they spread.

With every tear that graces stone,
A promise made, never alone.
Hands entwined, in prayer they stand,
Trusting in a higher hand.

Voices blend in gentle hymn,
Candles flicker, lights grow dim.
Eternity holds their dreams true,
For love eternal, always new.

In silence, trust begins to bloom,
Faith breaks forth from fleeting gloom.
In unison, hearts do sing,
Here in the unseen, hope takes wing.

Abandoned Prayers at Heaven's Gate

Upon the threshold, words unspoken,
Dreams dashed, yet hearts unbroken.
Fleeting moments on the breeze,
Reach for heaven, a soul's unease.

Lost in the echoes of the past,
In silence, forever cast.
Yet there lies a sacred fire,
From shattered hopes, desires inspire.

Through tears that fall like gentle rain,
We find strength amidst the pain.
With every prayer left unsaid,
God hears the longing of the dead.

In the quiet, spirit aches,
Yearning for what love forsakes.
At heaven's gate, the heart does wait,
For whispers soft that console fate.

An empty altar, a heavy sigh,
Yet faith will soar, will never die.
In every heart, that wish remains,
Eternal love, our soul's refrains.

The Spirit's Unvoiced Longing

In hush of night, the spirit cries,
For clarity amidst the lies.
Unseen hands reach for the stars,
Healing wounds, mending scars.

Whispers of truth, soft and fair,
Catch the echoes in the air.
In every sigh, a prayer unfolds,
Tales of warmth in the cold.

From depths of silence, fears arise,
Craving comfort in the skies.
With every heartbeat, hope ignites,
Guided by faith, through darkest nights.

A yearning deep, the spirit's plea,
For love that soars, a bond most free.
In the dance of shadows, still,
A promise made, through strength, we will.

Beneath the veil, the yearning stirs,
A tapestry of silent murmurs.
In unity, our hearts belong,
Harmonies of the spirit's song.

Epistles in the Shadows

From depths unknown, messages rise,
Written in silence, beneath the skies.
In shadows cast by faith's embrace,
Words of hope, a sacred space.

Each letter penned with trembling hands,
Carved in whispers, like shifting sands.
In every line, a spark ignites,
Guiding souls through lonely nights.

Testimonies of trials faced,
In darkest hours, grace embraced.
For every heart that feels alone,
Words of love sent from the throne.

As ink flows softly on the page,
Healing finds us, as we wage.
Against despair, we rise anew,
With every inked thought, we pursue.

In these letters of the soul,
Life's bitter truths make us whole.
Though shadows linger, light will steer,
In faith, we find the way most clear.